Take What You Need

.

TAKE WHAT YOU NEED

BY ZARA BAS

Take What You Need by Zara Bas

Copyright © 2022 by Zara Bas

All rights reserved.

ISBN: 9780645545562

Published by Zara Bas

Within these pages lies a map, yet the true key resides within you.

For those moments when you need just the right message:

Chapter 1 - *'Compassion'* serves to provide you with understanding, validation and warmth. Read this when you're needing a pick-me-up.

Chapter 2 - *'Reassurance'* is a compilation of essays and aphorisms written to put your mind at ease. Return to this safe space when nerves take over and the world is looking big and scary.

Chapter 3 - *'Hope'* is a collection of spirited and uplifting messages. This is where you'll find the motivation to persevere during those dark hours.

Chapter 4 - *'Growth'* presents an array of ideas for the soul-searcher on a self-development journey. If you're looking for wisdom and guidance along your exploration, here is where to land.

Chapter 5 - *'Healing'* dissects a number of hard-hitting truths and poses thought-provoking questions for your consideration. Here is where you will be challenged to gently face some of the deeper internal work.

Chapter 6 - *'Acceptance'* serves to normalise aspects of yourself and your connections you have shunned. Return to this section when you are ready to come to terms with where you are.

CONTENTS

Compassion

This is your sign to stop over-rationalizing poor treatment.

When you've been treated unfairly for long enough, you begin to internalise blame. You start to ask yourself if maybe it was you. Maybe you deserved such cruel punishment. You find yourself second-guessing your anger and hurt, despite its validity.

I am here to tell you it is not your job to soften your mistreatment. Give your mind a break from coming up with excuses for the way they've hurt you and let yourself acknowledge the unfairness of that pain.

Your love changes everything it touches.

Every drop of kindness you pour into the
universe ripples out in ways you do not see.

It makes sense that you feel lonely in a room full of people who do not truly see or hear you. It makes sense that you carry your loneliness from childhood, when persistent neglect made you feel invisible. It makes sense that you feel lonely when your vulnerability hasn't been welcomed.

But you must know that you are worthy of spaces that will embrace and understand you. You are worthy of the pursuit of true attachment.

A past filled with loneliness does not bar you from a future of connection.

Picture this:

You begin to see yourself through softer eyes. You show yourself the kind forgiveness of someone who loves you. You notice the child within you and speak to them with sweetness and leeway. You slowly start to love yourself the way you always deserved to be loved.

Hurt people don't always hurt people.

Sometimes hurt people are motivated to grow. Sometimes hurt people use their pain to find more empathy for others. Sometimes hurt people are more considerate and better able to spot the hidden signs of suffering. Sometimes hurt people bring more joy and love to their community. Hurt people don't have to hurt people.

So, to you who is hurting, remember your pain isn't necessarily contagious, but what you do with it is.

3 secrets about love in your twenties:

1. If you have to lie to keep it alive, it's already dead

2. There's no prize for neglecting your values to be the 'chill' partner
   (*psst the only prize is your discomfort*)

3. If they want you because they can't have you - you don't want them

Take What You Need

I see you.

I see how hard you try. I see the fight you put up. I see you struggling to get out of bed, trying to keep it all together. I see you reaching into yourself for every bit of effort you have left. I see you battling and I am here to let you know you are never alone in this fight.

I am here to tell you no matter how heavy it feels, *you won't be crushed by this.*

You are so brave for learning to love
yourself without a blueprint.

What a treasure it is to be moved so easily.

To cry during movies and develop feelings on first dates. How beautifully human of you to be brought to your knees by songs, books and paintings. Is it not a gift of great perception to feel love when you see your mother's hands kneading dough? To feel awe at the sight of a halo-encompassed moon? How brave it is to embrace your sensitivity, in a society that favours the jaded and cynical.

Pushing forwards even when you are
scared is the greatest form of resilience.

You don't have to be fearless
to make progress.

You are more than transactional.

You are worth relationships free of bargaining. Connections without an implicit 'I've done something for you, so you owe me' contract. You deserve care without strings attached. Affection without a down payment in favours. You deserve love that doesn't need to be earned.

There is more to you than what you can provide others.

Things not going your way
is an invitation
to try going a different way.

We look to our past to locate what happened that made us *'like this'*.

Far too often, we're left confused, searching for a defining moment. We forget that it may not be about what happened, but what was missing. The absence of a growing nutrient that should have been there, but wasn't - warmth, support, praise, forgiveness, unconditional affection.

Absence is a far more insidious form of damage, robbing us of the ability to neatly pinpoint the beginnings of our mental anguish. You must not blame yourself for not seeing an invisible blade.

The wound is evidence enough.

4 ways to develop deeper self-trust:

1. Allow yourself to makes mistakes without judgment

2. Commit to your ambitions and follow through on what you promise yourself

3. Don't 'should' yourself into a path laid by others

4. Shower yourself with self-reassurance

Take What You Need

No matter what you've been through, you are still equally worthy of a delicate and considerate love. No matter what baggage you carry or what adjustments you require.

Requesting your vulnerabilities be taken into account is not asking for too much.

Take What You Need

It's okay if your heart needs more time to
mend than you expected.

You have all the time in the world
to put yourself back together.

Take What You Need

Show me what you have to hide.

I want to see it. I want to hold it with affection. Show me all of your messiness and let me decide whether it is so. I'm sure I won't agree. At least give me a chance to view it with a pair of understanding eyes.

Maybe I can show you something you've yet to see for yourself.

Take What You Need

You deserve someone who won't need a
second chance to treat you right.

I'm sorry.

I'm sorry you hear internal alarm bells with the slightest shift in body language. I'm sorry your first thoughts are often to prepare for the worst. I'm sorry you were not taught what love looks like so you had to figure it out alone. I'm sorry that doing so meant experiencing all of what love isn't first. I'm sorry you couldn't find safety in places that should have felt like home. I'm sorry those who were supposed to be your refuge were the one's you were seeking refuge from.

I'm sorry.

No, you're not making a big deal out of nothing.

You're going through something. Something deep and dark and difficult. Something from the trenches of your mind. You are suffering something a second time in a new reality. No, you are not exaggerating how big it feels.

Leftover trauma stings with every new serving.

When you never got to see what healthy disagreement looks like, you feel on edge at the slightest hint of difference in opinion. But please know you are safe to be misunderstood now. You are safe to hold opposing views.

The mark of a good connection isn't a lack of difference. It's being able to open your mind to the idea that love can still live in the same space as two conflicting perspectives without threatening its strength.

Take What You Need

Dearest giver:

May you one day open yourself to receive.

You didn't deserve to be the scapegoat. You didn't deserve to carry all the anxiety by yourself. You didn't deserve the blame and projected insecurities others were not brave enough to shoulder themselves.

Remember that the burden was never yours to bear alone. Be free from the shadows of others' fears.

I hope you find someone
who adds to your life ,
rather than takes from it.

I hope they teach you
that love and suffering
are not synonyms.

Success is simply being alive.

You are successful today, because you exist. Not because of anything you have accomplished, but because being here, enduring and striving for peace is a success that overshadows any material accomplishment or lack there of.

You are bold enough to live and that is success.

5 reminders for when life feels dark:

1. There are moments ahead of you better than what you can currently imagine

2. This is an opportunity to trust the process and surrender to life's flow

3. You inspire others in ways you don't see

4. You've been down before and you've found a way through it

5. This is where the most beautiful transformations begin

The love you feel is not a flaw.

It is not something you need to hide or stifle. Nor an inconvenience to be ashamed of or apologetic over. Love with your heart on your sleeve and let it spill over in copious amounts. Let it breathe, expand and evolve. Give it free rein and never apologise for how big it is.

Let yourself love without seeing it as a weakness.

Maybe you're not where you want
to be just yet,

but there is a version of you
that would do anything
to be where you are now.

Just because growing pains are unavoidable, doesn't make them hurt any less.

Leaving things behind, moving through adversity and losing people along the way may be a part of your personal development, but it's okay to acknowledge the grief that comes with progress.

Your heartache is real and even if loss is a natural part of maturing, you are allowed to mourn the cost of it.

Take What You Need

You are worthy of love
that doesn't make you feel invisible.

You deserve to be seen in all your
glory and gore and adored just the same.

Take What You Need

Reassurance

Whether you stress about it or allow it to come to you with ease, it all falls into place on time. Even if you can't see it, it's all working in the background for your best interest. What might appear as a setback, could be an important step forward. Instead of getting swept up by the unknowns, ask yourself

'How could this situation be working in my favour?'

Take What You Need

It might take a while to get over,
but that doesn't mean you won't.

How beautiful is it that you tried anyway?

Even when your heart on a silver platter wasn't met with reciprocity, isn't it beautiful that you had the courage to offer it?

Even if it wasn't handled with the care you deserved, was it not beautiful to give yourself a chance?

Is it not proof that next time, in the right hands, you will be grounded in your ability to open yourself to another?

Take What You Need

You've been through enough.

You shouldn't have to *earn* peace.

Take What You Need

It's okay to be nervous.

It's okay to be anxious and scared. Your fear says nothing of what you can handle. It is purely a signal that you are stepping out of your comfort zone - where all the best growth happens.

Within the fear lies everything you've ever wanted. Here is where you find the change you've been hoping for. So lean in, even when you're frightened. Take that chance, despite being terrified.

A reminder of our shared humanity:

In the midst of self-doubt, we often convince ourselves that there must be something profoundly wrong with us, as if we are the only ones who bear flaws. But look around for a moment. Notice the incessant quest for perfection you're surrounded by. It's a collective pursuit that leaves us depleted and unsatisfied. It's a testament to the fact that we are all imperfect beings. This common thread binds us all and reminds us that being flawed is a natural part of the human experience.

Remember, you don't need to celebrate your flaws. You don't need to embrace them as parts of yourself you love - another sneaky form of perfectionism. All you need to do is accept them.

Take What You Need

You are allowed to want love.

You are allowed to wish for adoration. You are allowed to desire romance and partnership. Prioritizing love is not desperation, but your human search for connection.

The idea that you must fulfil all of your needs entirely independently does not account for the communal and social bonds we require to thrive. You must release your shame of dependence.

Take What You Need

Walking away
from what no longer serves you
leads you to what does.

You don't have to empathize with those who have hurt you to the point that you hurt yourself.

I know you care deeply for everyone and you're a master at explaining why they chose to act the way they did, but you're allowed to hold space for the pain they've caused without empathising it away.

Don't erase what you've had to endure solely because you understand where it came from.

Take What You Need

You teach the world what you want when you allow yourself to recognise your desires.

Your dreams exist for good reason. In some shape or form you are meant to pursue, align and embody them. You are called to embark on the discovery of their meaning as they lead you towards your authentic purpose. It is your job to stay open to the possibility of your wishes unfolding.

Beautiful beginnings come
out of stagnant things falling apart.

The love was real
because it was always yours to feel
not for anyone else to define.

Take What You Need

To that person stuck in an anxious loop:

You have been through enormous obstacles and have come out the other side every time. This time is no different. Trust me when I tell you - you are capable of more than you believe, even if it doesn't feel like it right now. The stories and limitations your bleakest moments whisper to you are simply your mind's attempt at protecting you, but they are not reality. Those worst case scenarios you're scanning through are nothing more than unreliable predictions.

You are in control of your own narrative. You are allowed to change it at any time.

It wasn't a mistake, it was part of your journey.

It wasn't wasted time, it was time spent identifying your true desires.

It wasn't useless, for you bring new knowledge with you as a result.

You don't need to 'toughen up'
you just need to be around people
who value your softness.

Take What You Need

This period of feeling stuck brings with it a
hidden gift -

the art of stillness, hibernation, and
patience.

If you lost someone who took your love for granted, you didn't lose.

You gained peace, freedom, time to explore, and the opportunity for someone who will cherish you properly. What you lost is nights spent crying yourself to sleep. You lost the feeling of being small and pandering to someone who doesn't see you. You lost begging to be treated with decency and the anxiety of never really knowing where you stand.

The loss you experience when you let go of connections that don't serve you brings you closer to peace.

Take What You Need

Choosing kindness doesn't mean forgoing assertiveness.

You can be considerate and respectful while holding tightly to the value of your needs and expressing your thoughts clearly. In fact, true kindness requires assertiveness. It requires you to be brave and honest instead of hiding your feelings for a false sense of harmony.

Every trial you have faced
has taught you to better care
for your broken parts.

Take What You Need

To the quiet observer:

Your presence is still noticed and appreciated.
You are not so easily forgotten.
Not invisible or unimportant.
Your silence draws the right people to you.

Going through the motions might lead you somewhere you're meant to be.

No matter how small of a step you are taking, it might be just the one that needed to fall into place at this time. The universe conspires in mysterious ways to guide you forward and it is your duty not to cut that journey short.

"Listen to your intuition!" they say, but how can you distinguish between intuition and anxiety?

What comes to you when your mind and body are at ease is that deep inner knowing worth your attention. It is calm, steady and grounded in the present. What urgently tugs at you when you're braced to escape or attack is the distorted voice of fear. It fixates on future what-ifs and spirals into overthinking.

Intuition is a quiet, but certain whisper.

Anxiety is a desperate plea for relief.

It hurts because it was hurtful,
not because you were '*weak*'.

Take What You Need

You don't need to constantly push yourself to be something better.

It's okay to spend time appreciating where you are right now. It's also okay if you need time to grieve and you're not ready or willing to make moves towards 'better' just yet. You don't have to be perpetually progressing.

Standing still for a bit might just be more productive than forcing yourself forwards.

Sometimes a situation
that will bring you so many new blessings
looks a lot like a curse at first.

Take What You Need

You are a full human being and you deserve to be loved in full.

Not just in your happiness, but also through your sadness. Through your anxieties and boundaries. You deserve to be loved not just when it is easy, but in all of your humanity.

Take What You Need

Let me tell you a secret, all the effort you're putting in is not in vain.

You're going to make something out of this. All that you are working for; building; toiling away at - it's going to work out. Your efforts will be rewarded in time and in unexpected gifts.

There is purpose and meaning behind what you do, even if you don't know it yet.

Take What You Need

Kindness will crack you open
and force you to see all your inner light.

Take What You Need

It was brave of you to keep the doors open for a chance at love.

You were full of grit and tenacity to give it a try. Regardless of how long it lasted, it was worth the practice. It was worth the depth of understanding you found for yourself. The time you gave them wasn't wasted, but an opportunity to exercise vulnerability.

Take What You Need

You are on the right path, because it is yours.

Even when you've disregarded the directions of another, hit a dead end or struggle to see across hills up ahead. Whether you have to take hundreds of detours, or backtrack for miles, the path you're on is correct, because it is yours.

Take What You Need

Hope

If you're on a healing journey you must remember that hope is not a given but a practice.

Too often we rely on hope to find us when we must go out in search of it. Hope is a skill to be cultivated, a daily exercise in the belief that things do get better. Hope is a muscle to be strengthened over time, practiced in the quiet hours of melancholy.

Do not wait for hope to find you when you're capable of creating it yourself.

Take What You Need

I know you miss who you were before the trauma. I know you grieve who you could have been without it. Honour that loss, but don't forget that you now have the freedom to create a new layer of yourself.

In your growth, you will discover the power to heal and reclaim your life in ways you may not have imagined. You are liberated from the ties of how you previously defined yourself. Use this space to explore and redefine what it means to be you. Your capacity for self-realization is limitless.

When you've learnt how to pull yourself
out of a dark place alone,
beyond that,
nothing is impossible.

Take What You Need

Trust me when I tell you love will find you when it's ready.

It will arrange itself in your life exactly as it's supposed to, no struggle or strain required. You won't need to force or chase it, as it will weave its way effortlessly to you. Take a deep breath, let go and allow it to come to you, knowing it's already on its way.

You will do more than just survive.

Beyond your awareness, your courage will grow as you make changes you never thought possible. You will get over that person and break free from old habits keeping you stuck in the past. As your heart heals, you will happen upon phases of motivation leading you to embrace new beginnings. Your path will look different to what you had mapped out, but it will be yours.

One day you will look back and be proud to see you did *more* than just survive.

How to prepare for the best:

1. Believe that it is possible

2. Leave your heart open to receive

3. Notice what is working in your favour
   (*no matter how small*)

It's all yours.

All of it.

Everything this world has to offer is in your hands - laughter, connection, adventure, spirit. Grasp it, hold it, cradle it. Take it all with you - the good and the bad, the lessons and their teachings. It was all put here for you to alchemise into your own wild journey. So step forward with courage.

The world is waiting for you.

Life has a profound way of
sending signs not to give up,
but you must keep looking for them.

New beginnings:

When it feels like everything is falling apart, remember that you are being given building blocks to put back together in a formation far more fulfilling than before.

Take What You Need

The worst is over now.

Take a deep breath, release any physical tension you're holding and let the weight fall off your shoulders. It's done. You're on the other side of this and from here on out it keeps getting better.

You did it.

You made it.

Imagine how much peace you could have
if you started entertaining hopeful
'what if's
and putting less stock
into worrisome predictions.

Take What You Need

You will face this, as you always have.

With courage or with fear,
you will continue anyway.

Take What You Need

Love doesn't always end in heartbreak.

I know what you've been through could only leave you expecting the worst, but you won't hurt indefinitely. There are people who will love you well. Who will love you unconditionally and teach you to believe again. There are places and life events that will be warm to you this time.

Don't pack up your heart just yet.

Take What You Need

There's enough time for you to become
all you wanted to be.

If you're feeling stuck, *I need you to know there is a path through this.*

It may be hidden just out of view, but it is there guiding you forward. Around the corner are breakthroughs you have yet to stumble upon, patiently waiting for you to take that leap of faith ahead. Remember, this temporary phase of being stuck is just a part of your journey, urging you toward transformative change.

If you can love someone
who gave you so little,
imagine how much
you could learn to love yourself.

Love doesn't just come to you when you least expect it. Love finds you when you search for it in the every-day.

Love is in dinner parties with friends on a Tuesday and the stranger who smiled at you on the street. Love is in a text from someone you care about and links to videos you think they might like. Love is in song lyrics and a pet curling in your lap. It's an excited infant waving at you and sharing half an umbrella. There are endless little ways to love and be loved if you only take a moment to let them live within you.

If you pay a little extra attention, you might start to see all the small places love likes to hide.

3 reminders for tough days:

1. Even if you don't know it yet, you have a bigger purpose here

2. The beauty this situation will lead you to is still undiscovered

3. Struggling to find reasons to continue, doesn't mean there aren't any

Take What You Need

Let me tell you what I believe -

I think you are going to get through this even though right now you feel like you won't. I think you're going to come out of this stronger, more connected and with the knowledge that you can get through whatever your future throws at you next. I think you're braver than you know, stronger than you feel and in tune with your resilience.

I think you're going to make it.

'Good things don't happen to people like me'

And yet berries and honey exist. And yet you wake up slowly with the sun streaming through your curtains. And yet Spring fills the air with the scent of lavender and budding plum blossoms. And yet you can dip your hands in water, feeling it flow through your fingers, reminding you of life's fluidity.

Nature's offerings remind us that good things are not reserved for others. They are all around, waiting to be noticed.

This year is about finding joy everywhere.

Step on crunchy leaves and peel an orange in the shower because it smells good and it feels primal. Write them a love letter. Write yourself a love letter. Keep the Christmas lights up if they make you happy. Keep the whole tree up. Hold hands if you're brave enough and stay in your pajamas all day because they're comfy.

This is your year of bathing in the little joys.

Take What You Need

If you're scared to love again,
I'm here to tell you that
not all love will leave you
worse than it found you.

Take What You Need

If darkness can find a way in, then so can light.

Under cracks in tiles and brick and through an unclosed window. Through movement and transition, an opening of a door. Through the slits in the floorboards and covered in soot down the chimney. The light creeps just as stealthily as the dark.

6 small comforts when hope is hard to find:

1. Slow mornings and sleep-ins

2. Clean sheets still warm from the dryer

3. Art that expresses everything you can't put into words

4. Showering after a long day

5. Candles that smell like cherished memories

6. Comfort foods that remind you of childhood

Take What You Need

Fear doesn't mean
that what's happening right now
isn't for your greatest benefit.

Take What You Need

Leave yourself room
to be pleasantly surprised
by what life might bring you next.

There are people who will love you in all the ways those who hurt you couldn't.

There is so much love and healing ahead of you still. You have yet to meet some of your sweetest connections. Many of your cold and dark spaces will be met with compassion by those you may have never expected to understand.

You must hold hope for a future filled with corrective experiences.

Take What You Need

Relax into the knowledge that
everything you need
is on its way to you.

For the person feeling like it will never get better:

I am here to tell you it does.

You will feel the shadows start to rise up and out of you when you show them compassion. Your eyes will well with tears of relief. Every step you take will feel a bit lighter, easier, ready. Ready to receive, ready for something new now that there is a vacant room inside you. One that was previously inhabited by pain, anger, and resentment will be decorated with golden light - harmony and ease. The persistent fog of hopelessness lifts to reveal so much lush growth and healing beneath.

You may not see it now, but it has been growing there all along.

Take What You Need

It's your turn for life to gaze upon you
kindly.

Take What You Need

Growth

Choosing emotional health is going to be uncomfortable at first.

It's going to feel unpleasant to be vulnerable while in a disagreement, instead of shielding through blame and defensiveness. It's going to be uncomfortable when you start feeling distrustful, but actively choose not to seek excessive reassurance. It's going to be unsettling to confront that which you're avoiding. It's going to be uncomfortable when you're wanting to replay the pain over and over but instead tell yourself to '*stop*'.

Choosing emotional health is going to be uncomfortable, but as you consciously break free from outdated patterns of protecting yourself, you begin the empowering journey of growth and emotional liberation.

Take What You Need

Sometimes it's a waiting game.

Sometimes you need to let time pass before
you see the image in front of you clearly.

Take What You Need

When you're used to being hurt, you look for pain everywhere.

You search for signs of abandonment and mistrust like a hawk. When you've been hurt repeatedly, your threshold of tolerance for missteps and misunderstandings diminishes. But in shrinking your tolerance, you might be missing out on gratifying connections.

You might be cutting people off too quickly, before giving them a chance to rewrite your expectations.

Freedom looks a lot like pain at first.

Freedom is rock bottom - a place to rebuild entirely fresh.

Freedom is relationships ending - space for more satisfying future connections.

Freedom is loneliness - a chance to get to know yourself better.

You're not going to want to hear this, but -

real love is going to cost you your peace at times.

Real love comes with conflict and differences in opinions. Real love holds space for anger, fear and unhappiness. Real love will test your patience and require you to be vulnerable in the most vulgar ways possible. It will rip your outer shell open with ease and poke at your soft innards. But it will also make you grow in ways you could never have expected. It will allow you such security you have the ability to truly reach out and expand into areas you thought weren't for you.

Real love is going to cost you your peace occasionally, but it will bring you closer to true harmony.

Take What You Need

May you find the courage to be flawed
in a culture of perfection.

Growth is going to require you to take the shame out of your coping mechanisms.

It makes sense that you reach for your phone or isolate yourself to avoid discomfort. It makes sense that you'd rather choose what feels good in place of being with your anxiety. You must begin to see your avoidance with the compassion it deserves - a sincere effort at safeguarding you from pain.

When you soften your self-judgment, you give yourself a chance to explore alternatives.

Take What You Need

When someone tells you to just
'get over it'

what they are telling you is they do not
possess the emotional maturity to hold
space for the entire range of healthy, but
uncomfortable emotions.

This is your year of seizing the life in front of you.

No more waiting to be someone else, somewhere else. No more saving the good candles for special occasions and waiting for Monday to start fresh. This is your year of accepting where you are now, however that looks.

This if your year free of self-imposed limitations.

5 hard truths about growth:

1. All the best things in life will require you to make sacrifices

2. Discomfort is not optional, it's mandatory

3. If you don't face yourself at some point, you will run forever

4. It will force you to leave behind parts of your identity that no longer fit

5. You will have to give up your need for control

Imagine how different your life could be if your ultimate quest was contentment over happiness.

Imagine if you made peace with this moment, settling on a feeling of long-term fulfilment rather than waiting on unpredictable bouts of joy. Imagine the release of all that pressure to be better, breathing in a sense of ease in where you are now.

Take What You Need

If you spend your time
looking for what you're missing,
you will always find it.

What if you stopped seeing conflict as drama and instead recognise it as love.

Approaching someone with disagreement is an act of great trust and affection. It is proof that you believe the listener to be mature enough to hear what you have to say. It's an honest attempt to fight for a better future together. An indication that you believe the relationship to be worth the work.

Take What You Need

When you find healthy love
you can't keep looking back
on a toxic past for guidance.

Take What You Need

Your power lies in embracing life's seasons.

As time passes, you witness relationships ebb and flow between seasons of closeness and distance. You observe periods of motivation and rest within your passions. Emotional seasons of melancholy and optimism come and go like summer green and autumn gold.

With experience, you understand that every season is sent to teach you something. It's here you learn the power of asking,

'What is this season teaching me? What hidden gifts does it hold?'.

Take What You Need

The beauty of self-love
is your opportunity to fall
for every new version of yourself
as you grow.

You must stop forcing meaning onto healthy emotions.

You do not need to smile through the pain or look for silver linings. You don't need to avoid your anger or sadness as if it's something to be ashamed of. What makes an emotion 'bad' is the meaning you give to it. It is neutral until you place a story on top. You decide how to label the emotions that flow through you. Know that neutrality is always an option.

Take What You Need

In an age of scrolling, swiping and eyes glued to a screen, the most rebellious thing you can do is to take back your time, attention and drive for authentic connection.

You revolt by *choosing* where to spend your energy, noticing when it is being stolen.

Take What You Need

I hope you don't feel the pressure to justify
every unfortunate event with a lesson.

Not everything has a hidden meaning.

3 ways to tell you've grown:

1. You hold space for nuance and complexity

2. You understand that opposing ideas can exist at once in peace

3. In a safe setting you move *towards* discomfort instead of *away* from it

If you love someone who has been hurt before, *please be patient.*

Let them play out the war in their head while you stay by their side. Understand that even with the best of intentions, you will unintentionally trigger them in places that are still raw. Know that while they might see your role as accidental, they will have to fight tooth and nail against the past.

If you love someone who has been hurt before, *please be gentle.*

Their memories make love scary and their dedication to you will require them to grapple with that fear. Let them tackle their apprehensions at their own pace and offer a gentle hand when they're ready.

If you love someone who has been hurt before, *please know that it is worth it.*

Transparent conversations
deepen good connections.

Honesty stabilises the right soul ties and
dissolves the wrong ones.

Jealousy can be a profound teacher.

Behind its insecurity, it illuminates our greatest desires. It can be transformed into a roadmap. With the assistance of gratitude, jealousy can provide a guiding hand. We can appreciate what we have and see clearly where we would like to be going and with a bit of further inspection - *how we can get there.*

Take What You Need

While your journey may have begun
with hardship,

it doesn't need to continue for you to grow.

Take What You Need

How do you find happiness?

You search for magic every day. You look at how the sunlight hits the water and makes it glow in the shower. You watch steam rise from warm drinks and dust dance in the light. You find meaning not in how much you can do or achieve, but how much you can feel and share with those who matter. You accept that the house, the car, a new city or a job may provide temporary relief but it is just that - *temporary.*

You find happiness when you look at what you normally glaze over. Your lack of fulfilment is the distance between you and perceiving all the magic that surrounds you.

Take What You Need

There are people you have yet to meet
who will bring out new parts of you.

Learning about yourself
doesn't happen within a vacuum,
but by experiencing context.

Take What You Need

You simply do not need to compare your journey with anyone else's.

We are all going in our own directions. Whether yours has brought you everything you desire yet is unrelated to those of others. You have not seen the obstacles along their journey, nor what they lost to get there. If you had, you might find you'd appreciate your own more.

Comparison will not help you take those steps further. It will only rob you of experiencing along the way, as your eyes are too busy taking in the sights on someone else's path, missing your own.

Take What You Need

You continue to return
to dysfunctional attachments
because you're looking for
the parts of yourself you gave them.

Growth is more than feeling better…

It's getting to know yourself better. It's knowing what you won't look past again. It's developing a state of calm and believing that things are working in your favour even when it feels like you've taken 10 steps backwards. It's knowing those 10 steps are a necessary part of your journey and taking them with confidence.

Beautiful things happen when you start
being more of yourself and less of what
you think others want you to be.

Take What You Need

Healing

Take What You Need

This is your sign to stop convincing people to care for you when they've shown you they don't.

You deserve to be around people who don't need to be convinced of your value. You shouldn't have to prove your worth, especially to those who are committed to undervaluing it.

You deserve to motivate yourself
through kindness instead of shame.

You can love someone, but you can't force them to grow.

Some people will not be ready to meet you at your level of self-reflection. The people you love might not understand your dedication to healing, nor will they see the value in it. While it may be painful and lonely to accept, let them be where they are.

It is your responsibility to love others, not change them.

Before you react, give yourself a generous amount time.

Before you make up your mind, let it sit for a bit. Allow it to cool off and watch as it subsides - from boil, to simmer, lukewarm to cold. Let yourself acclimate. Sleep on it.

The decision you make in a heated moment won't be the one you would have chosen had you given yourself time.

Insecurity is an unmet need.

The need for a secure sense of self. A safe home to come back to. Insecurity is not a thing of shame. An ugly and disfigured thing. Instead it is a call to return to ourselves and bolster our internal resources. To build more safety into our base through self-compassion and patience.

We heal our insecurities through listening without judgment and meeting ourselves with a tender curiosity.

I hope today:

- You're in a place where you no longer google 'how to keep them interested'

- You don't pine after those who are unclear in their intentions

- You don't check to see if they saw your last message

- You don't cancel plans on the off chance they finally get back to you about that vague and non-committal opportunity to 'chill'

Take What You Need

People who love you care about how you feel.

They care about how their actions impact you.
They care about what makes you uncomfortable.
People who love you care about your
boundaries. They care about how they speak to
you. They care when you say 'no'. People who
love you don't leave you wondering. They don't
pretend not to notice when they've hurt you.
They don't disregard what you feel for their
own gain.

People who love you make it clear they care.
They make sure that their love doesn't come at
your expense.

Take What You Need

If you have grown used to being eaten up
and spit back out in the name of 'love',

you will always search
for those with sharp teeth.

If I could give you one tip for avoiding heartache it would be this:

Be with someone who is just as invested in giving to you, as you are to them.

Look for someone who sees your excitement and doubles it. Don't settle for glazed eyes and 'mhmm's when you explain something that you burn white hot for. Find someone who notices your bids for connection and cares enough to try to meet them. Find someone who values the way you see the world and attempts to embrace it with the same enthusiasm.

Just because you love them
doesn't mean it's healthy for you
to be with them.

Take What You Need

A sip of water is enough for someone dying of thirst.

When you're accustomed to emotional deprivation and neglect, you will hold tightly to any sliver of care. While you deserve oceans, you will settle for drops, accepting affection in inconsistent waves. You will hold onto unhealthy connections and weather the stress, shame and hits to your self-esteem they bring for a taste of tenderness.

But you have the power to break free from this pattern. Within you is a deep spring of self-love waiting to be nurtured. As you explore its depths you find yourself attracted to the kind of fulfilling warmth you were always entitled to.

Watch how love arrives in abundance when you change your internal landscape.

You see beauty in everything.

Why do you make an exception for yourself?

If you keep going back to something that is hurting you, I want you to know that you are not alone.

We've all searched for love in cold, uninterested hands. We've all stuck around in draining dead-end places, hoping something will change. Escaping painful patterns takes an immense amount of courage and you may not be aware of it yet, but the fact that you have read this far means you are already gathering strength to make a change.

In case you were never allowed to be angry as a child and now you,

'just don't get angry'…

Anger can be a useful, healthy and safe emotion as long as you're not hurting yourself or others.

Take What You Need

Don't disconnect from yourself
to connect with someone else.

If matching someone's energy
requires you to lose yourself,
it is not a connection worth pursuing.

Maturity is letting people in who have shown themselves to be trustworthy.

It's giving them a chance to treat you the way you have always hoped to be treated. Maturity is acknowledging your fear of being hurt and having the bravery to face it anyway, with the understanding that authentic connection cannot exist without risk.

Are you projecting
the love you deserve
onto others?

Questions for finding peace during setbacks:

- Is there a lighter way to think about this process?

- What are the limiting beliefs being unearthed that I am resistant to let go of?

- I have been challenged before. How did I manage last time?

- How is this assisting my growth?

- Can I see this situation with curiosity and openness instead of avoiding the pain it brings?

Take What You Need

In case you forgot - life is about experimenting.

Not everything you do has to be a revolutionary action. You're allowed to play and explore and discover. You're allowed to produce things that fail along the way. You're allowed to try all manner of activities without skill.

Life is, after all, a testing ground where joy is cultivated in the process, despite the outcome.

Take What You Need

When you bite your tongue,
you're the one who bleeds.

Take What You Need

How do you know it's not love?

It makes you feel small. It prompts you to start every expression of need with an apology. It leaves you constantly depleted of energy as you pour yourself into it, with a lack of reciprocity. It feels confusing and uncertain, fragile and inconsistent. It takes when it's convenient and bails when it's not.

This is how you know it's *not* love.

Take What You Need

You're going to want to give up sometimes.

Not because it's right for you, but because you are human. Because being human is exhausting at times and you'll think that if you just give up, you'll finally be able to rest.

But the reality is you can give yourself permission to rest now and along the way. You can allow yourself moments to be disillusioned by your goals with the understanding that they will pass.

Remember, there was a reason you started in the first place. Take time to recharge before you count yourself out.

A question for fixers:

Who put you in charge of saving everyone
and why didn't they include you?

Take What You Need

The hard truth is *unrealistic expectations serve to keep your suffering alive.*

When all is well, you will seek perfection to prove it is not, because you are used to things going poorly. You become so familiar with hardship and disappointment that you see it even when it is not present.

Allow yourself to experience happiness without doubt, for you are worthy of harmony. It's time to let go of the fear that it will be taken from you if you surrender to it.

I used to think love was enough for a lasting connection.

Now I look back fondly on how naive I was. If I have learnt anything it is that love is not nearly enough. It takes a solid commitment, sacrifice, compassion, boundaries, and understanding. It requires you to grow, to have the ability to introspect and reflect on your soft spots. It forces you to adapt and learn and consistently work on yourself. It begs you to bring your best and healthiest self forward. It asks you to be patient and kind when you're at your most emotionally-charged. To listen when you want to talk. It takes action and effort and by god it will teach you your limits.

It will show you who you are - the hills you're willing to die on and the mountains you will move. Most of all it asks you not to give up when that little inner voice tries to trick you into believing you'll be abandoned or hurt again if you don't take the easy way out before they do.

If you loved yourself more,
what would you do differently?

Take What You Need

Sometimes loving yourself means leaving.

It means getting hurt in the process and choosing the hard choice over the easy one. Sometimes you have to give up on people for your own sake. You have to come to terms with the fact that you can't help people who don't want to be helped. You must choose to see when your love's lack of interest in doing the work deprives you of all you deserve.

Take What You Need

I know it feels impossible,
but you can and you will heal.

Take What You Need

You must be cautious not to identity too closely with your fears and anxieties.

For so long I introduced myself as my anxieties, that I began to believe to my very core that I lacked the resilience to stand up to my fears. I became so closely acquainted with worry until bravery and courage seemed like unknown strangers. I cast them aside, far more confident in my ability to cower than fight.

So take it from me - you are more courageous than you know, but you must at least give yourself the chance to believe it to be so.

Take What You Need

Your journey towards healing cannot stop at discovering the root of the problem.

Now that you've bought awareness to the distortions, it's time to take action to correct them. From here you have the power to begin surrounding yourself with what you never received - placing yourself in the way of loving support, respect and understanding. This is where you transform introspective knowledge into purpose.

This is how you heal.

Take What You Need

Acceptance

The secret to feeling better is this:

Suffering can only survive for as long as
you keep resisting your current state.

Take What You Need

To feel empowered you must fully embody who you are, even in spaces where that might mean you're left on the fringe. There's something incredibly powerful about not pandering to what the world tells you to be and fiercely protecting your heart's desires.

To feel empowered you must be brave enough to embrace your authenticity in the face of disapproval.

'Weird' is contextual.

If you feel like you don't fit in - it's likely not because there's something wrong with you, but that the environment you're in doesn't suit you.

To accept yourself when others have not is
the most rebellious form of self-love.

You don't need to change yourself to be loveable.

You need to change how you think of yourself.

You need to recognise that even if you weren't always treated like it, you've always been worth loving. You've always carried little bits of sunshine and star-matter with you, shining light on everything you interact with.

You need to understand that being loveable doesn't mean being someone else - it's shifting what you see in yourself.

A gentle reminder for the over-thinker:

The more you let go,
the more the answers will find you.

Take What You Need

You are finding yourself in your lack of need to be found by others.

You're not going to be everyone's taste and that is something to celebrate. When you start to tap into the discrepancies between you and those you don't belong with, you will learn to trust more in your own opinion - your internal compass. You will leave the crowds that amplify your loneliness. You will make space for places and hearts that embrace you wholly.

If you aren't to everyone's liking, you have succeeded in connecting with yourself.

Take What You Need

Don't search for answers in big feelings.

Impassioned answers are generally a manifestation of your pain and not your actualised self. Once the urgency passes, a path forward always shows itself.

The most loving home you will ever build
is the one within yourself.

Take What You Need

Let them lose you if:

- Their first response to you telling them how they hurt you is to explain why you're wrong

- You don't show up on their priority list

- Their affection is inconsistent

- They can't meet your needs after you've laid them out clearly

Take What You Need

Love doesn't take more than it gives.

Love evens out the score. Love says, 'I see you can only give 20% today so I will give 80%, with the knowledge that you would do the same for me if I needed it'. Love replenishes and rejuvenates two dedicated souls. It is not easy or without work, but it is an eternal spring of offering.

You deserve at least as much love as you give, for true love gives more than it takes.

Take What You Need

Maybe you're not ready to see it yet.

Maybe you're still telling yourself this is what you want, even if you know intuitively it's not. And maybe that is how it has to be right now, because it will reveal itself to you when it is time. Maybe you're still covering your eyes and blocking your ears and this is just a part of your journey right now until it is time for you to gain clarity.

Take What You Need

You don't have to settle for someone
whose wounds
wound you.

Take What You Need

The harsh reality is you cannot love
someone into being the person
you need them to be.

Your love is enough.

Your love is expansive, transformative, and pure. It is generous and ever-understanding. Someone's ability to hurt you does not mean you are giving away too much of your heart, but that you are brave enough to try.

It is safe to feel all the love you have.

Take What You Need

Even though they knew how much
their actions would hurt you,
they chose them anyway.

That is all the closure you will ever need.

The difference between a healthy and unhealthy relationship is that both will inevitably cause pain, but in a healthy relationship there's a concerted effort towards repair.

Being a good partner doesn't end at doting on someone. It's not limited to showering each other with love when you're both on the same page or when it's easiest. It's knowing when and how to take accountability. It's leaving room for difference to exist. It's setting aside your ego in order to make apologies and repair a priority.

Take What You Need

If someone is telling you
they can't meet your needs,
it's not your job to convince them to.

Accept their limits and go elsewhere.

Take What You Need

Holding on to unhealed patterns doesn't serve you any longer.

It doesn't put you in a position to accept and receive the care you deserve. It doesn't allow you to find true peace. Holding on to unhealed patterns keeps you begging for the bare minimum and waiting for things to change without change being enacted. It drains you of your power while you're permanently stuck in limbo waiting for things to get better.

It is time to observe what is calling for your attention and accept that there is work to be done.

This is your reminder to take that first action towards change.

Take What You Need

Lessons from healthy love:

- You won't be left with doubt about their feelings or intentions

- It will require growth and learning from both parties

- It will (safely) trigger your past wounds and challenge you to heal

- You won't be made to feel like a burden

- Your feelings and the effects of their actions on you will be considered

- You will still be disappointed at times

- You will have to learn to communicate to listen, not just to be heard

Take What You Need

Decide whether you can love them
as they show up *today*.

Not for who they promise to be *tomorrow*.

This might be hard to hear but until you bring awareness to it, the pain doesn't stop.

I know you want to ignore it, but you have to see it in all its light before it can be understood and actioned upon to dissipate. You have to confront it - look it dead in the eyes and say 'I'm ready to witness you now' even when it causes your stomach to churn.

You have to see it to release it.

It's okay to want to be loved
with the same intensity that you love.

Take What You Need

What a deeply powerful rebellion to say to yourself,

'I love you and I am going to care for you to the best of my ability, no matter how confusing or painful that might be'.

Hear me out - strong people know when to give up.

Yes, the 'never give up' mentality might work for some, but for many it is invalidating. Disregarding our limits and pushing ourselves beyond our safe capacity can do more harm than good. Sometimes a lack of acceptance of these limits only furthers our suffering as we continuously ignore signs and symptoms from our bodies and minds that persistence isn't helpful.

Strong people put in every effort, but they also know when acceptance is the greatest effort they can give.

Take What You Need

Sometimes you have to spend time
being unhappy where you are,
before you figure out
which direction you want to go.

Instead of invalidating your hardships by focusing only on the silver lining, could you alternatively accept that things are allowed to just be terrible from time to time?

Could you take a break from the temptation to put a positive spin on things? Could you recognise that part of self-compassion involves allowing yourself to grieve what could have been and accepting how painful this current reality is?

Acknowledging that this outcome was not what you wanted, won't dash all chances at hope, but it will grant you the opportunity to truly process and heal.

Embracing your sensitivity
is a radical act of authenticity.

A love letter to wallflowers:

In a world that favours the most social among us, you hold hidden powers. Your rich inner world is full of introspection and quiet reflection. You notice what is easily overlooked and find a sense of ease in solitude. Here you have access to creativity and thoughtful contemplation, allowing you to discover the complexities of the human existence. Your words, few and far between, hold weight and are steeped in meaning. You are The Listener, The Deep-Thinker, The Empathic-Supporter.

The world benefits from your quiet wisdom and keen observation.

Take What You Need

Let go of what you don't know.

Surrender to the unrevealed secrets of your life. Sometimes all you can do is embrace the uncertainty. Stare at it directly in the face knowing you can't change it, but no matter what happens you will make it through.

As frightening as it may be, you are brave enough to sit with this.

Take What You Need

Dearest reader,

Thank you for allowing me to share my words with you. I truly hope that you found both comfort and perspective throughout this book.

Please consider leaving a review on Amazon or Goodreads. I am ever-grateful to receive your feedback and follow your journey.

ABOUT THE AUTHOR

Zara Bas is an Australian best-selling author sharing her exploration of self-love. After completing a Bachelor of Psychology and Master of Neuroscience, Zara was inspired to delve deeper into the minds of the tender-hearted. Through her craft she strives to create an accessible space to feel, release and process.

Zara released her first book of modern poetic-style prose '*I Have to Tell You Something*' in 2022 which quickly became a best-seller in its category internationally. This collection explores her learnings on relationships, break-ups, self-esteem, and purpose. In her second book '*This Time You Save Yourself*', Zara expands upon this journey with a focus on heartbreak, mistreatment and recovery. She continues to write and share her work across social media hoping to motivate others to get to know themselves in greater depth.

Instagram: @zarabaspoetry
Tiktok: @zarabaspoetry

MORE FROM ZARA BAS

I Have to Tell You Something (2022)

Soft and hard truths written from the most tender depths of a healing heart, these are the words your inner child needs to hear.

This Time You Save Yourself (2022)

An anthem to those who have been mistreated by the ones who should have held you tightest

Made in United States
North Haven, CT
26 September 2023